Voices of the Rainforest

Manning

Britta Granström

W
FRANKLIN WATTS
LONDON•SYDNEY

Contents

Authors' note: most of the animals and plants in this book come from the Amazon rainforest and may be found in other rainforests as well. We only say where an animal or plant is found if it is never in the Amazon.

A rainforest home

Welcome to the rainforest. It's huge, hot and
very wet. It rains nearly every day so clouds
hang over it like steam over a hot bath.
The forest is deep, dense and very dark.
You could get lost – unless you lived here . . .

Come with us
and explore the
rainforest.

Rainforests grow around the tropics – the area on Earth either side of the Equator. The South American rainforest is the size of Europe, and the rainforest in Africa isn't much smaller. Look at the map to see where else in the world you find rainforests.

Tropic of Cancer

Equator

Tropic of Capricorn

Rainforest

We'll show you our home.

Over half the world's wildlife live with us in the rainforest.

Teeming with life!

Thousands and thousands of different kinds, or species, of animal and plant live in the rainforest. Even today people are finding new ones.

From jaguars in South America to gorillas in Africa; from rafflesia in Indonesia to bower birds in Australia; tree frogs, brazil nuts, colobus monkeys, fig trees, harpy eagles, macaws, people – the world's rainforests are teeming with life.

We live together in a huge house deep in the forest.

People of the forest

The people of the world's rainforests are clever, shy and secretive. They make their homes, tools and clothes from the forest that surrounds them.

Each rainforest tribe has their own way of living in the forest. Some live in groups in one big house.

Other tribes prefer village life. In the villages of one tribe, the men live together in a hut at the centre.

The people of the rainforest have taught us about many of the foods and medicines that we use today. These people are gathering brazil nuts.

Mum paints my face. It takes ages – but looks fantastic!

Many rainforest people paint their bodies and faces with dye made from the genipap fruit. Each tribe has its own special styles. The paints will last a few weeks before fading away.

9

Hunt and gather

Rainforest people hunt wild animals and gather food like roots and berries from the forest. Some tribes also plant 'gardens' of herbs and vegetables.

My blowpipe fires a dart. I've dipped it in poison!

The poison the hunters use is curare. It comes from a forest vine. It relaxes the muscles – now doctors use it to help them operate on people's muscles more easily.

Lots of things are tasty in the rainforest – roasted tortoise, forest pig with wild honey, crunchy roots, fruit and fish!

Some rainforest people use long arrows to shoot fish or tree-top animals.

In Indonesia and South America, people collect latex from rubber trees. Done carefully, it doesn't harm the trees.

People dig out tree trunks to make canoes.

Papaya is my favourite fruit. I love wild honey comb, too!

We live among giants – trees that stretch up to the sky!

Giant trees

The kings of the rainforest are its giant trees. Some can grow over 60 metres tall. Their branches and leaves form a roof over the forest. We call this roof the canopy.

Butterflies feed in the canopy by day.

There may be 600,000 flowers on a big tree with over 150 litres of nectar in them. This sugary liquid is food for millions of insects, birds and bats.

Leaves are a plant's food factory. The green stuff in them traps energy from sunlight and uses it to make food from water and carbon dioxide in the air.

When plants make their food, they give out the oxygen that we need to breathe.

The canopy gets 90 per cent of the sunlight. It creates a deep shade in the forest below.

Rainforest giants grow so tall and heavy they need to have huge buttress roots to hold them up.

Our giants give us a gift - the oxygen we breathe!

Moths feed at night.

Canopy world

Hundreds of different animals live in the tree-top world of the canopy: from butterflies, lizards and tree frogs to parrots, sloths and monkeys. Many of them never touch the ground.

Tree-top animals climb, jump, glide and swing!

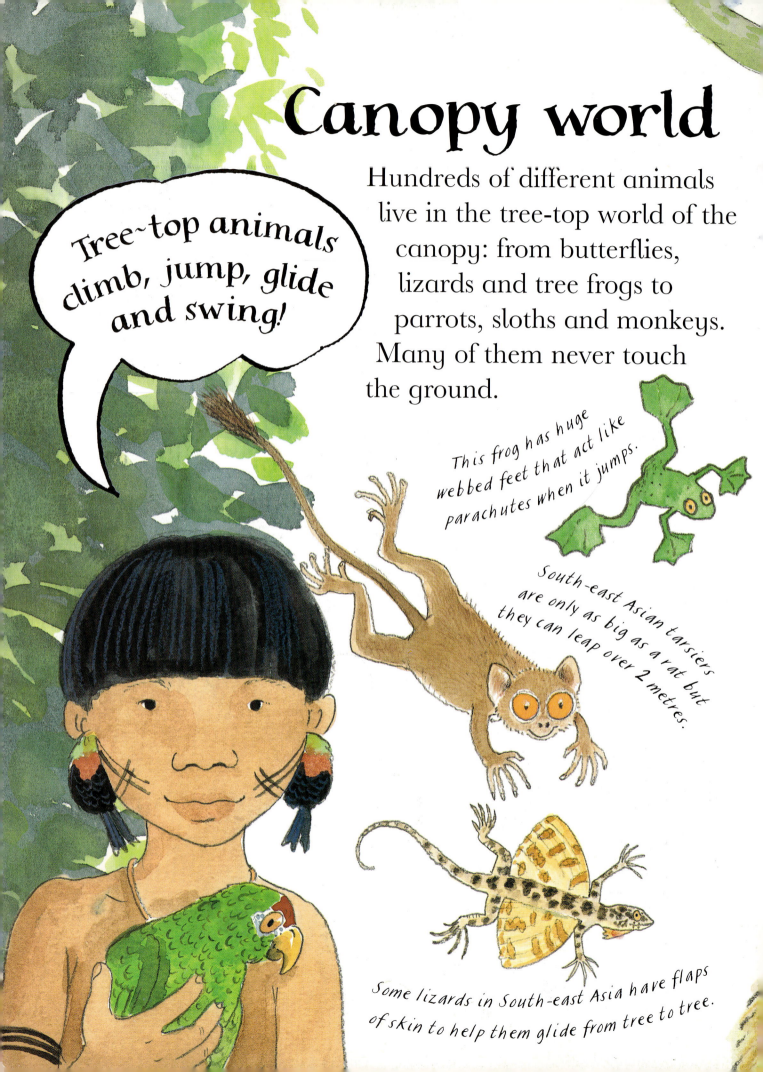

This frog has huge webbed feet that act like parachutes when it jumps.

South-east Asian tarsiers are only as big as a rat but they can leap over 2 metres.

Some lizards in South-east Asia have flaps of skin to help them glide from tree to tree.

Squirrel monkeys, like many tree dwellers, have 'prehensile tails' that they use like an extra hand.

Sloths spend a lot of time upside down - and so their fur grows upside down too, allowing rain to run off easily!

African Colobus monkeys are experts at leaping from branch to branch.

Gibbons are from South-east Asia. They can judge distance perfectly with their sharp eyes as they swing through the trees.

15

The understorey

Beneath the canopy is the dark understorey. It is wet and steamy! Palms, ferns and small trees grow here, with vines twining around them. Look out for frogs, jaguars, and thousands of insects, snakes and lizards.

Liana vines make good ladders. You can swing on them, too!

Lianas twist and climb among the trees - path ways for small animals and insects like these leaf-cutter ants.

Jaguars hide on low branches to sleep – or to jump down on any tasty-looking creatures feeding on the forest floor.

Plants like bromeliads can have rainwater pools of up to **54** litres of water between their leaves! Coatimundi and other tree-dwellers visit them to drink and bathe. Some frogs and crabs even rear their young in these tree-based ponds.

The brightly coloured stripes on a poison arrow frog say: 'Danger – don't eat me!'

Forest floor

We move silently through the forest without snapping a twig.

Hardly any sunlight reaches the forest floor and very few plants grow. It's covered in rotting leaves and wood. This leaf litter is crawling with insects, snakes and spiders.

The rafflesia of South-east Asia has the largest flower in the world. It smells like rotten meat to attract flies.

Tiny poison-dart frogs hop through the leaf litter.

Lowland gorillas forage in the African rainforest.

Pitcher plants grow in South-east Asia and Australia. They can't get all goodness they need to grow properly from the poor soil. Instead, the plants trap and digest insects. Frogs often hide in them for a free meal!

Tarantulas and fierce ants hunt the insects scurrying across the floor.

Tapirs forage for food on the forest floor with their stripy babies.

Old trees

Rainforest trees can live for 200 years but, as they die and rot, they become both homes and food for many forest animals.

A dead tree quickly becomes **a food store** for wildlife!

This tree boa squeezes its prey to death in its coils.

Termites live in – and eat – old trees.

Female hornbills nest in tree holes in Africa and Asia. They 'cement' themselves in with mud to be safe from predators. The male hornbills bring them their food.

As trees rot, they are broken down by fungi and by tunnelling insects, passing the goodness in the plant back into the soil. And then back into more plants.

Strangler figs grow around other trees, gradually killing them. By the time the tree inside rots away, the fig has grown tall enough to reach the sunlight in the canopy.

Figs grow tasty fruit – lots of animals eat them including me.

21

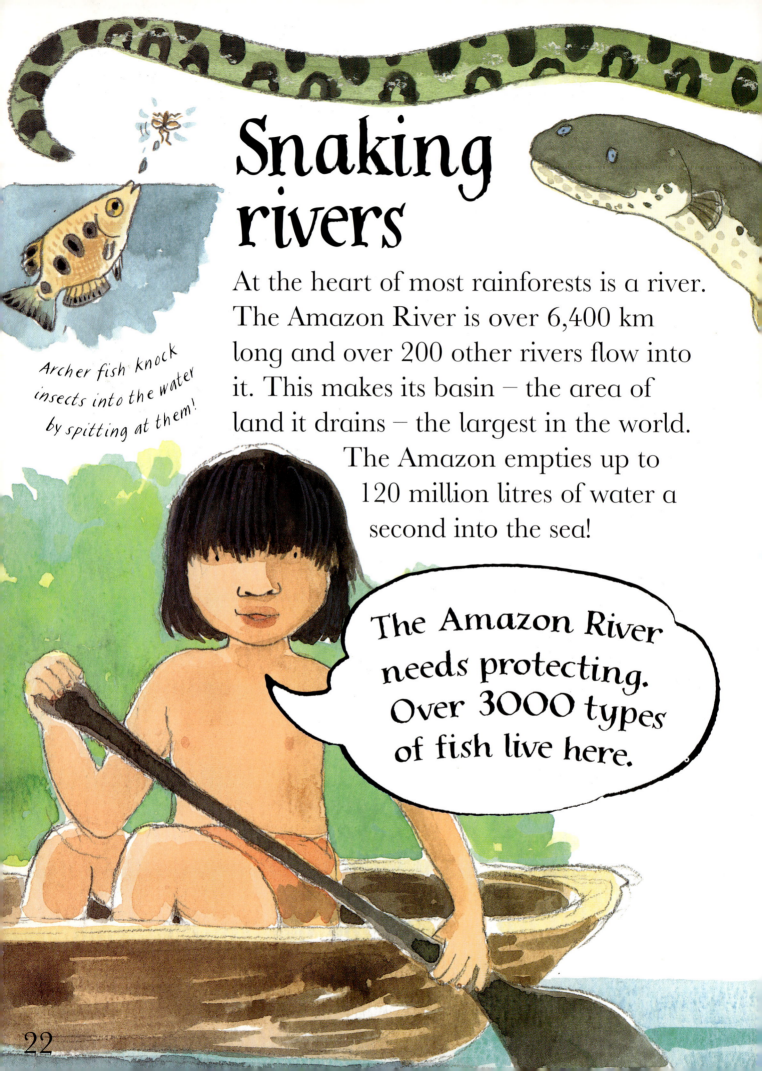

Snaking rivers

At the heart of most rainforests is a river. The Amazon River is over 6,400 km long and over 200 other rivers flow into it. This makes its basin – the area of land it drains – the largest in the world. The Amazon empties up to 120 million litres of water a second into the sea!

Archer fish knock insects into the water by spitting at them!

The Amazon River needs protecting. Over 3000 types of fish live here.

The biggest snake in the world, the anaconda, can swallow a deer whole!

The Amazon holds 20 per cent of all the fresh water in the world.

Electric eels stun their prey with an electric shock.

Piranhas' teeth are like saw blades. They can strip a large animal down to its skeleton in just a few minutes.

Caymans are a sort of crocodile that hunt fish - and any other animals that come near the river.

This jacana is trotting across giant lily pads.

Zizz!

Noise and colour

In the thick forest animals communicate by sound or with colourful markings. By day animals sing and whoop, birds flash colourful wings. At sunset, night animals take over; tree frogs call, insects sing, bats natter, jaguars moan . . .

The cock-of-the-rock adds colour to the forest floor.

eeek!

The forest is a noisy place but I can tell who makes each sound.

Plip!

Frogs come in every colour of the rainbow. Even when you can't see them in the dark, you can hear them – they sing all night.

Riches of the rainforest

Jojoba nut oil makes creams and perfumes.

Rainforests are rich in natural resources: wood, rubber, food and wildlife. Many plants can be used as medicines to help us all, in fact new ones are still being discovered!

Bananas

Brazil nuts

Pineapple

These are just a few of many fruits from the rainforest: avocado, coconut, guava, mango, orange, papaya, passion fruit and tangerines.

Chocolate comes from cacao seeds.

Tea tree oil is used to make shampoo, soap and antiseptic cream.

Latex can be made into many things – from raincoats to rubber balls!

Most rainforests grow in poor countries and cutting down the forests for wood seems a quick way to make money.

Poor farmers follow the roads made by loggers and try to farm – but the crops quickly fail as the goodness in the thin forest soil is used up. Without the trees to hold it together, the soil is easily washed away. The rainforest can't regrow even when the farmers leave.

Why destroy our rainforests? They give us so much.

Cattle ranchers cut and burn the trees to make way for thousands of cattle. One day you might eat one – as a beef burger in your local fast-food restaurant!

27

Rainforests forever!

Plants and animals are the real riches of the rainforest. Many are in danger of extinction – dying out forever. To save them, we must find a way to make the most of the forests without destroying them. Rainforest people have always lived this way. Let's listen to the voices of the rainforest before it's too late.

The rainforest doesn't belong to us. We belong to the forest.

The rainforest is a gift we must all treasure.

29

You and the rainforest

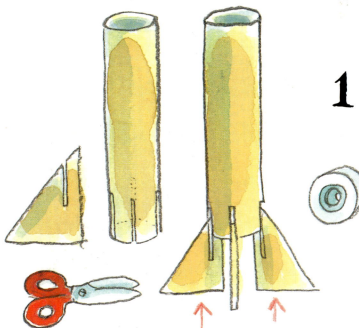

1 Create a forest of giant trees with buttress roots for rainforest animals to hide in.

Use kitchen paper tubes for the trunks and triangles of cardboard for the roots. Make the leaves from scrunched up tissue paper.

2

Make a blowpipe by rolling up and taping a large piece of paper or newspaper. Screw up paper to make balls that fit the pipe. Stand up some toys or empty plastic bottles, take aim and blow! Can you knock them down?

3 Pretend to be rainforest animals: try being super slow sloths, or playing 'eagle hunt monkey' tag . . .

Empty plastic bottles make a good target for your blowpipe!

4 You can help save the rainforest by joing a conservation group like WWF. Ask an adult to help you find out more about this group on the Internet (www.panda.org).

5 Make your own monkey chain copying this shape for each link.

6 Grow a pineapple. Ask an adult to cut off its crown with about 5 cm of the fruit. Scoop out any soft flesh and leave the crown upside down somewhere dark to dry for a day or so. Then plant the crown in a pot of soil and place it somewhere warm like a sunny window sill. Keep the soil damp and watch your plant slowly grow.

Index

This edition 2007

First published in 2004 by Franklin Watts, 338 Euston Road, London NW1 3BH

Franklin Watts Australia, Level 17/207 Kent Street, Sydney NSW 2000

The illustrations in this book have been drawn by Mick and Brita. Find out more about Mick and Brita on www.mickandbrita.com

Text and illustrations © 2004 Mick Manning and Brita Granström

Editor: Rachel Cooke
Art director: Jonathan Hair

A CIP catalogue record is available from the British Library.
Dewey classification: 577.34

ISBN 978 0 7496 7376 5

Printed in China

Franklin Watts is a division of Hachette Children's Books, an Hachette Livre UK company.

For Zane Foster